Wood Pellet Smoker and Grill Cookbook

The Art of Smoking Meat for Real Pitmasters, Ultimate Smoker Cookbook for Real Barbecue

By Roger Murphy

TABLE OF CONTENTS

INTRODUCTION **9**

WHY SMOKING **10**

CHAPTER 1 PORK **11**

    KOREAN PULLED PORK 11

    OVERNIGHT TAMARIND SPARE RIBS 14

    PORK CHOPS WITH GRILLED MANGO PINEAPPLE SALSA 17

    MEDITERANEAN MEATBALLS IN SPICY TOMATO SAUCE 19

    SMOKED PORK SAUSAGE WITH BISCUITS AND GRAVY 22

CHAPTER 2 HAM **25**

    HICKORY SMOKED HAM HOCKS 25

    PINEAPPLE BOURBON GLAZED HAM 28

    SWEET 'N SPICY GLAZED HOLIDAY HAM 30

    WHITE BEAN AND HAM SOUP 33

CHAPTER 3 LAMB **36**

    CHOCOLATE AND MINT LAMB 36

    LAMB MEATBALL CASSEROLE 38

    SLOW-ROASTED LAMB SHOULDER WITH HOMEMADE HARISSA 42

    TEXAS-STYLE LAMB SHOULDER CHOPS 45

CHAPTER 4 BEEF 47

    IRISH STOUT BRAISED CORNED BEEF IN WITH CABBAGE 47

    MEXICAN-STYLE BEEF NACHOS 50

    BACON AND EGG BREAKFAST BURGER 52

    BEEF SHORT RIB, TOMATO, AND POTATO STEW 54

    SPAGHETTI BOLOGNESE 57

    HONEY-APPLE BBQ RIBS 60

CHAPTER 5 CHICKEN 63

    APPLE-WOOD SMOKED CHICKEN BURGERS 63

    APRICOT CHIPOTLE GLAZED CHICKEN 66

    HONEY GINGER HOT CHICKEN WINGS 69

    RED CURRY MARINATED CHICKEN 71

CHAPTER 6 TURKEY 74

    SMOKED WILD TURKEY JERKY 74

    TURKEY MADRAS 76

    TURKEY MEATLOAF WITH GREEN CHILIES 79

CHAPTER 7 FISH 82

    FENNEL & SWEET PEPPER STUFFED SMOKED TROUT 82

    LINGCOD WITH CHERRY TOMATOES AND OLIVES 84

    MAPLE SMOKED RED SNAPPER STEAKS 86

CHAPTER 8 SEAFOOD 88

- BARBECUE SHRIMP 88
- CRAB AND SHRIMP DIP 91
- SCALLOP PASTA 94

CHAPTER 9 VEGETABLES 97

- GERMAN-STYLE SAUERKRAUT WITH APPLES 97
- GRILLED BROCCOLI WITH LIME BUTTER 99
- GRILLED VEGETABLE SALAD 101

CHAPTER 10 GAME 103

- FROG LEGS WITH CREOLE DIPPING SAUCE 103
- GRILLED DUCK BREAST 106
- ROASTED ELK PEPPER POPPERS 108

CHAPTER 11 SMOKING MEAT 111

- Wood Pellet Using Tips 111
- Selecting a Smoker 113
- Choose your wood 113
- Select the right meat 115
- Find the right temperature 115
- The core difference between cold and hot smoking 116
- The basic preparations 117

The core elements of smoking! 118

CONCLUSION **119**

MY BOOKS **120**

Get Your FREE Gift *132*

INTRODUCTION

The ultimate how-to guide for smoking all types of pork, beef, ham, lamb, vegetables, fish poultry, and game. This book on smoking meats for beginners is the guide to mastering the low and slow art of smoking meats at your home. This guide is an essential book for beginners who want to smoke meat without needing expert help from others. This book offers detailed guidance obtained by years of smoking meat, includes clear instructions and step-by-step directions for every recipe. This is the only guide you will ever need to professionally smoke a variety of meat. The book includes photographs of every finished meal to make your job easier. Whether you are a beginner meat smoker or looking to go beyond the basics, the book gives you the tools and tips you need to start that perfectly smoked meat.

<u>WHY SMOKING</u>

Smoking is generally used as one of the cooking methods nowadays. The food enriches in protein such as meat would spoil quickly, if cooked for a longer period of time with modern cooking techniques. Whereas, Smoking is a low & slow process of cooking the meat. Where there is a smoke, there is a flavor. With white smoke, you can boost the flavor of your food.

In addition to this statement, you can preserve the nutrition present in the food as well. This is flexible & one of the oldest techniques of making food. It's essential for you to brush the marinade over your food while you cook and let the miracle happen. The only thing you need to do is to add a handful of fresh coals or wood chips as and when required. Just taste your regular grilled meat and a smoked meat, you yourself would find the difference. Remember one thing i.e. "Smoking is an art". With a little time & practice, even you can become an expert. Once you become an expert with smoking technique, believe me, you would never look for other cooking techniques. To find one which smoking technique works for you, you must experiment with different woods & cooking methods. Just cook the meat over indirect heat source & cook it for hours. When smoking your meats, it's very important that you let the smoke to escape & move around.

CHAPTER 1
PORK

KOREAN PULLED PORK

(TOTAL COOK TIME 16 HOURS 30 MINUTES)

INGREDIENTS FOR 6-8 SERVINGS

THE MEAT

- 1 boneless pork shoulder (8-lb, 3.6-kgs)

THE SEASONING

- Soy sauce - ¾ cup
- Hoisin sauce - ⅓ cup
- Gochujang - ⅓ cup
- Rice vinegar – ¼ cup
- Tomato ketchup - ⅓ cup
- Toasted sesame oil – ¼ cup
- Honey – 3 tablespoons
- Black pepper – ½ teaspoon
- Chinese five-spice – 1 tablespoon
- 6 garlic cloves (peeled, chopped)
- Fresh ginger (peeled and chopped) – ¼ cup

THE SAUCE

- Canola oil – 1 tablespoon
- Diced onion – ½ cup
- Chicken stock – 1 cup
- Gochujang – 2 tablespoons
- Tomato ketchup – ½ cup
- Soy sauce - 2 tablespoons
- Honey – 2 tablespoons
- Chinese five-spice powder – 1½ teaspoons
- Toasted sesame oil – 2 teaspoons
- Rice vinegar – 2 tablespoons

THE GRILL

- Preheat your grill to 240°F (115°C) with the lid closed for between 12-15 minutes

METHOD

1. First, prepare the seasoning. In a bowl, combine the soy sauce, hoisin sauce, gochujang, rice vinegar, tomato ketchup, sesame oil, honey, black pepper, 5-spice, garlic, and ginger.
2. Add the seasoning to a large ziplock bag along with the pork shoulder. Seal the bag and massage gently to coat in the marinade evenly. Chill overnight.
3. Take the marinated pork out of the bag and place it directly on the grill.
4. Smoke for 8-10 hours until the meat registers an internal temperature of 195°F (90°C). Take the pork off the grill and transfer to a baking pan. Cover loosely with aluminum foil and allow to rest for 10 minutes.
5. In the meantime, prepare the BBQ sauce. Warm the canola oil in a saucepan over moderate heat. Add the onion and sauté until softened.
6. Next, stir in the chicken stock, gochujang, tomato ketchup, soy sauce, honey, and Chinese five-spice. Cook for 8-10 minutes until the sauce has reduced a little. Take off the heat and then stir in the sesame oil and vinegar.
7. Shred the cooked pork and serve with the BBQ sauce.

OVERNIGHT TAMARIND SPARE RIBS

(TOTAL COOK TIME 15 HOURS 30 MINUTES)

INGREDIENTS FOR 8 SERVINGS

THE MEAT

- 2 racks fresh pork spare ribs, membranes removed

THE SLATHER

- Tamarind juice concentrate – 3 tablespoons
- Honey – 1 tablespoon
- Apple cider vinegar – 1 tablespoon

THE RUB

- Light brown sugar – 3 tablespoons
- Freshly ground black pepper – 3 tablespoons
- Kosher salt – 2 tablespoons
- Garlic powder – 1 tablespoon
- Onion powder – 1 tablespoon

THE SODA MOP

- Cola, any brand – ½ cup
- Apple cider vinegar – ¼ cup

THE SMOKE

- When you are ready to cook preheat a smoker to 225°F (107°C)
- Alder wood chips work well with this recipe

METHOD

1. First, make the slather. Stir together the tamarind juice concentrate, honey, and apple cider vinegar in a small bowl.
2. Brush the ribs all over with a thick layer of the slather, removing any excess.
3. Prepare the rub: combine the brown sugar, black pepper, salt, garlic powder, and onion powder in a small bowl. Coat the wet ribs with the dry rub, patting to create a crust.
4. Cover and allow to rest overnight.
5. The following day, place the ribs, bone-side facing downwards and smoke.
6. Create a mop by combining the cola and apple cider vinegar in a bowl. You will need to apply the mop every 7-8 hours, or until the meat registers 165°F (74°C), and the meat falls easily apart.
7. Cover with foil and allow to rest for 20 minutes before serving.
8. Serve and enjoy.

PORK CHOPS WITH GRILLED MANGO PINEAPPLE SALSA

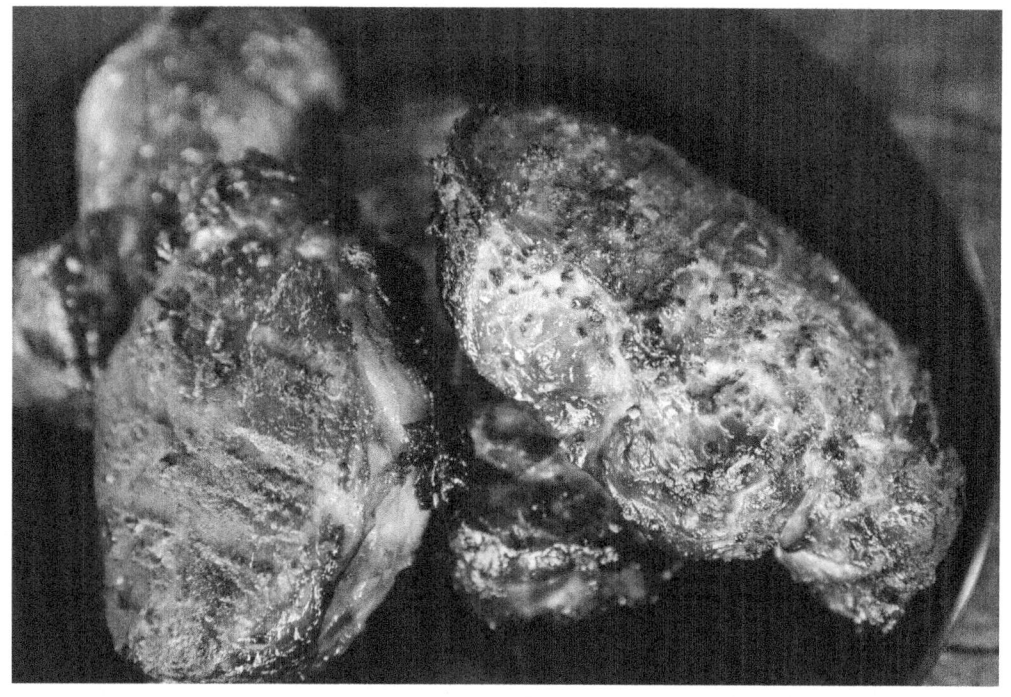

(TOTAL COOK TIME 1 HOUR)

INGREDIENTS FOR 2-4 SERVINGS

THE MEAT

- 3 (1-lb, 454-gms) thick-cut, bone-in pork chops

THE SEASONING

- Pork rub – 2 tablespoons
- BBQ sauce, of choice – ¼ cup

THE SALSA
- ½ pineapple (peeled, cored, diced)
- 1 ripe mango (peeled and diced)
- ½ red onion (peeled, sliced)
- 2 red bell pepper (deseeded, diced)
- 2 tbsp fresh cilantro (chopped)
- 1 garlic cloves (peeled, minced)
- Juice of 1 medium lime
- Salt and black pepper

THE GRILL
- Preheat your grill to 450°F (232°C) with the lid closed for between 12-15 minutes
- We recommend apple wood for this recipe

METHOD
1. Season the pork chops all over with the pork rub. Chill for half an hour.
2. In the meantime, prepare the salsa. Combine the pineapple, mango, onion, bell pepper, cilantro, garlic, lime juice, salt, and black pepper. Set aside until ready to serve.
3. Place the chops on the preheated grill and cook for 8-9 minutes, flip and brush the exposed side generously with BBQ sauce. Cook for another 8-9 minutes or until the meat registers an internal temperature of 165°F (74°C).
4. Allow the chops to rest for a few minutes before serving with the salsa.

MEDITTERANEAN MEATBALLS IN SPICY TOMATO SAUCE

(TOTAL COOK TIME 1 HOUR 50 MINUTES)

INGREDIENTS FOR 4-6 SERVINGS

THE MEAT

- Ground pork (1-lbs, 0.45-kgs)
- Ground chorizo (0.5-lbs, 0.23-kgs)

THE MEATBALLS

- Milk – ¼ cup
- 2 medium-size eggs, beaten
- Fresh garlic, minced – 1 tablespoon
- Yellow onion, minced – 2 tablespoons
- Breadcrumbs – 1 cup
- Paprika – 2 teaspoons
- Fresh Italian parsley, finely chopped – 2 tablespoons
- Parmesan cheese, freshly grated – 2 tablespoons + additional

THE SAUCE

- Olive oil – 1 tablespoon
- ½ yellow onion, peeled and diced
- Fresh garlic, minced – 2 tablespoons
- Canned diced tomatoes (2-lbs, 0.9-kgs)
- Jarred piquillo peppers, diced – 2 tablespoons
- Granulated sugar – 2 tablespoons
- Paprika – 2 teaspoons
- Salt – 1 teaspoon
- Chipotle chili powder – ½ teaspoon
- Green onions, chopped – 2 tablespoons

THE SMOKE

- Preheat your smoker to 300° F (105°C)
- Use your favorite wood pellets for this recipe

METHOD

1. In a small-size bowl, whisk the milk with the eggs. Put to one side.
2. In a second, larger mixing bowl, using clean hands, combine the ground pork with the ground chorizo. Add the garlic, onion, breadcrumbs, paprika, parsley, and 2 tablespoons freshly grated Parmesan.
3. Add the milk-egg mixture to the meat mixture and incorporate. Roll the mixture into small evenly-sized meatballs.
4. Arrange the meatballs in a single layer on the smoker grid and cook for approximately 60 minutes. You will need to rotate the meatballs halfway through cooking. The meat is sufficiently cooked when it registers an internal temperature of 160° F (71°C).
5. While the meatballs are cooking, prepare the tomato sauce.
6. In a pan over medium heat, add the olive oil. When the oil is hot, add the onion and sauté for 2-3 minutes, until softened.
7. Next, add the garlic and sauté until golden, for 2-3 minutes.
8. Pour in the canned tomatoes, and add the diced peppers, sugar, paprika, salt, and chipotle powder. Bring to a simmer for 20 minutes.
9. Using a handheld stick blender, blitz the tomato-chipotle mixture until almost smooth, with some small-size chunks still remaining.
10. When the meatballs have smoked for 60 minutes, transfer them to a disposable aluminum tray. Pour the tomato sauce over the top of the meatballs, and smoke for an additional 20 minutes.
11. When you are ready to serve, remove from the smoker, garnish with more grated Parmesan cheese and serve.

SMOKED PORK SAUSAGE WITH BISCUITS AND GRAVY

(TOTAL COOK TIME 1 HOUR 25 MINUTES)

INGREDIENTS FOR 2-3 SERVINGS

THE MEAT

- Tube pork sausage, casings removed (12-ozs, 28.35-gms)

THE BISCUITS

- Flour – 2 cups
- Salt – ½ teaspoons
- Baking powder – 3 teaspoons
- Butter, cold and cubed– ½ cup
- Whole milk – ¾ cup

THE GRAVY

- Flour – 2 tablespoons
- Whole milk – 2 cups
- Black pepper

THE SMOKE

- When you are ready to beginning cooking, with the lid open set your pellet grill to 'smoke' and establish the fire; for 5 minutes
- Use mesquite wood pellets

METHOD

1. Place the pork sausage on the preheated grill and smoke for 30 minutes to one hour.
2. In the meantime, make the biscuits. Cover a baking sheet with parchment paper and set to one side.

3. Combine the flour, salt, and baking powder, in a bowl. Cut in the butter cubes until the mixture is breadcrumby. Incorporate the milk gradually until the mixture forms a firm dough.
4. Lightly flour your worktop. Tip the dough out onto the worktop and knead until the dough comes together and is smooth.
5. Gently shape the dough into a ½ -ins (1.25-cms) thick disc. Using round biscuit cutters, cut discs out of the dough. Place the discs on the baking sheet.
6. Take the cooked sausage off the grill and turn to 'grill.' Set the temperature to 450°F (232°C), close the lid, and allow it to come to heat.
7. Place the baking sheet of biscuits on the grill and cook for 10-12 minutes until risen and pale golden.
8. In a skillet over moderately high heat, sauté the sausage for several minutes until browned and cooked through. Take the sausage out of the skillet and set aside in a bowl. Do not drain the fat from the skillet.
9. Add the flour to the skillet and whisk to combine it with the fat— Cook for 60 seconds before whisking in the milk. Bring the mixture to a boil then turn down to a simmer. Cook for a couple of minutes before returning the sausage to the skillet.
10. Season to taste with black pepper.
11. Slice the cooked biscuits in half and top with the sausage gravy.
12. Serve!

CHAPTER 2
HAM

HICKORY SMOKED HAM HOCKS

(TOTAL COOK TIME 50 HOURS 30 MINUTES)

INGREDIENTS FOR 16 SERVINGS

THE MEAT

- 8 ham hocks (2-lbs, 0.9-kgs) each

THE BRINE

- Boiling water, filtered (8.5-ltr, 9-qts)
- Kosher salt – 2½ cups
- Brown sugar – 1½ cups
- Whole black peppercorns – 3 teaspoons
- 6 bay leaves

THE SMOKE

- Preheat the smoker to 250°F (120°C)
- Add hickory wood chips to the side tray. Pour water into the bowl

METHOD

1. First, brine the ham hocks. Pour the boiling water into a deep-sided pan. Add the kosher salt, brown sugar, black peppercorns, and bay leaves. Stir thoroughly until the salt and sugar have entirely dissolved. Put to one side to cool.
2. Add each ham hock to a large-size ziplock bag and pour an equal amount of brining liquid into each bag to cover the meat. Seal the bag tightly.
3. Place the bags in a deep dish then transfer to the fridge for 24 hours.

4. Remove the ham hocks from the brine, rinse thoroughly under cold water, and using kitchen paper towels, pat dry.
5. Put a rack inside a sheet pan and place the ham hocks on top. Chill in the fridge for an additional 24 hours.
6. Put the ham hocks in the smoker, and with the vent open, cook for 2-4 hours. You will need to top-up the water and hickory wood chips every hour or so.
7. The ham hocks are sufficiently cooked when their internal temperature registers 160°F (70°C).

PINEAPPLE BOURBON GLAZED HAM

(TOTAL COOK TIME 5 HOURS 10 MINUTES)

INGREDIENTS FOR 14-16 SERVINGS

THE MEAT

- 1 spiral ready to eat ham (8-lbs, 3.6-kgs)

THE GLAZE

- Pineapple preserves (18-ozs, 0.5-kgs)
- Dark molasses – ⅓ cup
- Runny honey – 1 cup
- Bourbon – 1 cup
- Brown sugar – ½ cup
- Ground mustard – 1 tablespoon
- All-purpose rub - ½ cup

THE SMOKE

- When you are ready to smoke, preheat your smoker to 225°f (107°c)
- hickory wood chips are recommended for this recipe

METHOD

1. Over low heat, in a pan, combine the glaze ingredients (pineapple preserves, dark molasses, honey, bourbon, brown sugar, mustard, and all-purpose rub). Stir to 20-25 minutes, or until the glaze starts to thicken.
2. Take off the heat and allow the glaze to thicken as it cools.
3. Smoke the ham for 4-6 hours, to your preferred color is achieved. You will need to glaze every 10-15 minutes during the final 60 minutes of smoking.
4. Enjoy.

SWEET 'N SPICY GLAZED HOLIDAY HAM

(TOTAL COOK TIME 2 HOURS 10 MINUTES)

INGREDIENTS FOR 14-16 SERVINGS

THE MEAT

- 1 fully cooked, ready to eat, bone-in ham (8-lbs, 3.6-kgs)

THE RUB

- Dijon mustard, divided – 2 tablespoons
- Brown sugar, divided – ¼ cup

THE GLAZE

- Runny honey – 1 cup
- Brown sugar – ¾ cup
- Butter – 1 cup
- Dijon mustard – 1 tablespoon
- Ground cloves – 1 teaspoon
- Ground cinnamon – 1 teaspoon
- Pure Canadian maple syrup – 2 tablespoons

THE SMOKE

- Preheat your wood pellet grill to 300°F (149°C)

METHOD

1. Combine the rub ingredients in a small–size bowl. Coat the ham all over with the mustard-brown sugar rub.
2. Place the ham on the grill and cook for between 1½-2 hours until a meat thermometer inserted into the thickest part of the meat registers 165°F (74°C).
3. Next, prepare the glaze. In a saucepan, combine the honey with the brown sugar, butter, Dijon mustard, cloves, cinnamon, and maple syrup. Set over low heat, mix until the sugar dissolves, and on a low simmer, keep the glaze warm.
4. When the ham registers the required temperature, take it off the grill and cover it all over with the glaze. Set a small amount of the glaze to one side for serving.
5. Slice the ham and serve with a side of the remaining glaze.

WHITE BEAN AND HAM SOUP

(TOTAL COOK TIME 1 HOUR 40 MINUTES)

INGREDIENTS FOR 8-12 SERVINGS

THE MEAT

- 1 meaty ham bone

THE INGREDIENTS

- Olive oil – 1 tablespoon
- 1 onion, peeled and chopped
- 2 garlic cloves, peeled, crushed and minced
- 3 stalks of celery, diced
- Chicken broth – 4 cups
- Water – 4 cups
- 4 bouillon cubes
- 2 bay leaves
- 2 sprigs of thyme
- 1 bunch of sage
- Chinese 5 spice - ½ teaspoon
- 3 carrots, peeled and diced
- 3 (15-ozs, 425-gms) cans navy beans, drained and rinsed
- Diced ham – 1 cup
- 1 (15-ozs, 425-gms) can cannellini beans, drained and rinsed
- Salt and black pepper, to taste

THE SMOKE

- When you are ready to cook, set the grill to smoke and with the lid closed, preheat to 325°F (163 °C) for 10-15 minutes
- Mesquite wood chips are recommended for this recipe

METHOD

1. In a large Dutch oven, heat the oil.
2. Add the onion, followed by the garlic and celery. Cook, while stirring every 3 minutes, until the onions are translucent and softened.
3. Pour in the chicken broth along with the water. Add the bouillon, ham bones, bay leaves, thyme, sage, and Chinese 5-spice to the Dutch oven. Cover with a lid. Close the lid of the grill and increase the temperature to high heat.
4. As soon as the broth begins to simmer, increase the heat to 325°F (163°C) and allow to simmer while covered for 60 minutes.
5. Add the carrots and continue cooking for 15 minutes.
6. Add three cans of drained navy beans and the additional cup of diced ham. Cook for another 5-10 minutes.
7. Remove the soup from the smoker and take out the ham bones. Allow the bones to cool before you strip off the meat.
8. In the meantime, while the bone cools, in a food blender, blend the remaining can of beans with 1-2 cups of the soup broth.
9. Remove the bay leaves, sprigs of thyme and sage leaves—season to taste with salt and black pepper.
10. Enjoy.

CHAPTER 3
LAMB

CHOCOLATE AND MINT LAMB

(TOTAL COOK TIME 1 HOUR 30 MINUTES)

INGREDIENTS FOR 2-3 SERVINGS

THE MEAT

- 1 rack of lamb

THE RUB

- Olive oil – 2 tablespoons
- 2½ garlic cloves, peeled and minced
- Fresh chocolate mint leaves, minced – 2 tablespoons
- Juice and zest of 1 lemon
- Fresh parsley, minced – 1 tablespoon
- Black pepper – ½ teaspoon

THE GRILL

- Preheat the wood pellet grill to 300°F (149°C) with the lid closed for between 12-15 minutes

METHOD

1. In a bowl, combine the olive oil, garlic, chocolate mint, lemon juice, lemon zest, parsley, and black pepper to form a paste.
2. Slather the paste evenly over the lamb rack, reserve any excess paste.
3. Place the lamb on the grill and cook until it reaches an internal temperature of 130°F (54°C).
4. Take the lamb off the grill and transfer to a serving platter, cover loosely with aluminum foil.
5. Set your grill to open flame, and using tongs, sear the lamb over the flame until it reaches an internal temperature of 145°F (63°C).
6. Serve!

LAMB MEATBALL CASSEROLE

(TOTAL COOK TIME 1 HOUR 30 MINUTES)

INGREDIENTS FOR 4-6 SERVINGS

THE MEAT

- Ground lamb (1-lb, 454-gms)

THE SAUCE

- Olive oil – 2 tablespoons
- ½ yellow onion, peeled and minced
- 2 garlic cloves, peeled and minced
- Tomato sauce – 2 cups
- 8 plum tomatoes, peeled and chopped
- Dried basil – 1 teaspoon
- Dried oregano – 1 teaspoon
- Dried rosemary – ½ teaspoons
- Pitted black olives, chopped – ¼ cup
- Salt and black pepper

THE MEATBALLS

- ½ onion, peeled and diced
- 1 egg, beaten
- 3 garlic cloves, peeled and minced
- Kosher salt – 1½ teaspoons
- Fresh parsley, minced – ¼ cup
- Black pepper – 1 teaspoon
- Dried oregano – 1 teaspoon
- Dried rosemary – 1 teaspoon
- Dried basil – 1 teaspoon
- Panko breadcrumbs – ¼ cup
- Canola oil – 2 tablespoons

THE CASSEROLE

- Rotini noodles – 6 cups
- Nonstick cooking spray
- Parmesan cheese – ½ cup

THE GRILL

- When ready to cook the casserole, preheat the wood pellet frill to 350°F (177°C) with the lid closed for between 12-15 minutes

METHOD

1. First, prepare the sauce. In a skillet over moderate heat, warm the olive oil. Add the onion and sauté until translucent. Add the garlic and sauté another 60 seconds.
2. Next, add the tomato sauce, plum tomatoes, basil, oregano, and rosemary. Bring the sauce to a simmer and cook for half an hour, stirring occasionally.
3. Stir in the olives and season to taste with salt and black pepper.
4. Next, prepare the meatballs. Using clean hands, combine the ground lamb, onion, egg, garlic, salt, parsley, black pepper, oregano, rosemary, basil, and breadcrumbs. Roll the mixture into medium size balls.
5. In a skillet over moderately high heat, brown the meatballs on all sides in canola oil and cook until the meat registers an internal temperature of 165°F (74°C).
6. Cook the rotini pasta using packet instructions, drain.

7. To assemble the casserole. Spritz a casserole dish with nonstick spray. Toss the cooked and drained pasta with one cup of the prepared tomato sauce. And spoon into the casserole dish in an even layer.
8. Arrange the meatballs on top of the pasta. Pour over the remaining sauce and sprinkle over the parmesan.
9. Place the casserole in the grill on the lower rack and bake for 30 minutes, the sauce should be bubbling and the cheese melted.
10. Allow to rest for 5 minutes before serving.

SLOW-ROASTED LAMB SHOULDER WITH HOMEMADE HARISSA

(TOTAL COOK TIME 5 HOURS 30 MINUTES)

INGREDIENTS FOR 4-6 SERVINGS

THE MEAT

- Lamb shoulder roast on the bone (3-lb, 1.4-kgs)

THE RUB

- Coriander seeds – ¼ teaspoon
- Caraway seeds – ¼ teaspoon
- Dried mint – 1 teaspoon
- Cumin seeds – ¼ teaspoon
- Ancho chilies, deseeded and chopped (2-ozs, 57-gms)
- Sweet paprika – 1 tablespoon
- Fresh lemon juice – 1 tablespoon
- 2 cloves garlic
- Extra virgin olive oil – ¼ cup
- Salt

THE GRILL

- Start the wood pellet grill on smoke with the lid open for 4-5 minutes, until the fire is established
- Set the temperature to 325°F (163°C) with the lid closed for between 12-15 minutes
- We recommend cherry wood for this recipe

METHOD

1. Using a spice grinder, grind together the coriander, caraway, mint, and cumin seeds. Set aside for a moment.
2. Add the ancho chilies to a bowl and cover with water. Heat in the microwave for 2 minutes. Allow to cool before transferring the chilies to a blender along with 2 tablespoons of the cooking liquid.
3. Add the ground spices, paprika, lemon juice, garlic, 2 tablespoons olive oil, 1 tablespoon salt to the blender with the other ingredients and blitz to a puree.
4. Arrange the lamb in a roasting pan and rub the meat with ½ a cup of the paste. Set aside at room temperature for 2 hours.
5. Pour half a cup of water into the roasting pan and cover loosely with aluminum foil. Place in grill and cook for 2½ hours, you may need to top up the pan with water.
6. Turn off the grill, but let the meat stand for 20 minutes before taking it off the grill.
7. Use a fork to pull the lamb off the bone in large chunks. Serve the lamb with the remaining harissa sauce.

TEXAS-STYLE LAMB SHOULDER CHOPS

(TOTAL COOK TIME 5 HOURS)

INGREDIENTS FOR 4 SERVINGS

THE MEAT

- 4 lamb shoulder chops
- Extra-virgin olive oil
- Texas-style meat rub

THE BRINE

- Buttermilk – 4 cups
- Water, cold – 1 cup
- Coarse salt – ¼ cup

THE SMOKE

- Preheat your wood pellet grill to 240°f (115°c) and prepare for grilling with indirect heat. Fill the water pan with hot water
- We recommend cherry or apple wood chips for this recipe

METHOD

1. First, make the brine. Stir together the buttermilk and cold water in a measuring jug. Next, stir in salt until it completely dissolves.
2. Add the lamb chops to a ziplock bag and pour in the brine to cover the meat.
3. Chill the chops for 3-4 hours. Take the chops out of the brine. Discard the brine and rinse the chops.
4. Drizzle a little oil over both sides of the chops and use a pastry brush to spread the oil out evenly. Season both sides of the chops with Texas rub.
5. Place the chops on the smoker and cook for approximately 25 minutes until the meat registers an internal temperature of 110°F (43°C).
6. Allow to rest for a few minutes before serving.

CHAPTER 4
BEEF

IRISH STOUT BRAISED CORNED BEEF IN WITH CABBAGE

(TOTAL COOK TIME 8 HOURS 20 MINUTES)

INGREDIENTS FOR 4 SERVINGS

THE MEAT

- Corn beef brisket, flat cut (3-lbs, 1.36-kgs)

THE INGREDIENTS

- Irish stout – 1 cup
- 4 garlic cloves, peeled
- ½ onion, peeled
- 1 medium cabbage, cored and cut into wedges
- Dijon mustard – 2 tablespoons
- Dark brown sugar – 2 tablespoons

THE SMOKE

- Preheat the temperature of your pellet grill to 275°F (135°C)

METHOD

1. The morning of the day you want to prepare this dish, remove the brisket from its packaging and rinse well.
2. Place the meat in a stainless steel bowl and cover with cold water. Transfer to the fridge for 2 hours. Drain off the liquid and replace the water, return to the fridge for 2 hours. Drain once again and cover with cold water for another 2 hours.

3. Add the brisket to a cast-iron casserole pan with a tight-fitting lid. Pour half of the Irish stout around the meat so that the liquid comes halfway up the side of the meat.
4. Add the garlic and onion to the pan. Cover with the lid and put on the lowest rack of the preheated grill.
5. Braise for 1½-2hours until the meat registers 205 degrees F (96°C)
6. Remove the pan and increase the heat to 350 degrees F (177°C).
7. Remove the brisket from the braising pan and place it on an aluminum foil-covered pan. Add the wedges of cabbage into the pot, cover, and return, this time to the middle rack.
8. In a bowl, combine the mustard with the brown sugar to create a paste.
9. Spread the paste evenly over the top of the meat. Place it on an aluminum foil-wrapped sheet and position it on the grill alongside the pot containing the cabbage. Bake until the glaze is browned for 20-25 minutes. Using a slotted spoon remove from the pan.
10. Put the corned beef on a platter, and surround it with the cabbage.
11. Serve the corned beef with veggies of choice, and enjoy.

MEXICAN-STYLE BEEF NACHOS

(TOTAL COOK TIME 25 MINUTES)

INGREDIENTS FOR 6 SERVINGS

THE MEAT

- Ground beef (2-lbs, 0.9-kgs)

THE INGREDIENTS

- 2 large bags tortilla chips (18-ozs, 0.5-kgs) each
- 6 large green bell peppers, seeded and diced
- 6 large red or orange bell peppers, seed and diced
- Scallions, sliced – 1 cup
- Spanish red onion, peeled and diced – 1 cup
- Monterey Jack cheese, shredded – 6 cups
- Sour cream, to serve
- Mexican salsa, store-bought
- Guacamole, store-bought
- Tomatoes, chopped small

THE SMOKE

- Start the grill on smoke with the lid open establish a fire for 5 minutes
- Preheat the temperature to 350°F (177°C)

METHOD

1. In a cast-iron pan, arrange 2 layers of tortilla chips.
2. Layer with ground beef, bell pepper, scallions, red onion, and shredded Monterey Jack cheese.
3. Put the pan on the grill and cook for 8-10 minutes until the cheese melts.
4. Remove the pan from the grill and serve with sour cream, Mexican salsa, guacamole, and chopped tomatoes.
5. Dip in and enjoy.

BACON AND EGG BREAKFAST BURGER

(TOTAL COOK TIME 20 MINUTES)

INGREDIENTS FOR 2 SERVINGS

THE MEAT

- Lean ground chuck beef (8-ozs, 227-gms)
- 4 slices of cooked crisp bacon

THE BURGER

- Salt and freshly ground black pepper
- Olive oil
- 2 hamburger buns, split
- 2 slices American cheese
- 2 eggs, fried sunny-side up
- 2 hash browns, cooked and kept warm

THE SMOKE

- Set the grill to smoke and with the lid open establish a fire, for 4-5 minutes
- Preheat the temperature to 400°F (205°C)

METHOD

1. Divide the beef into two equal-size portions. Using clean hands, form the mixture into 2 patties. Season with salt and freshly ground black pepper.
2. Brush the grill grate with oil. Place the patties on top and grill for 3-4 minutes each side until cooked to your desired level of doneness.
3. Lightly toast the buns until golden.
4. Remove the burgers from the grill and place each one inside the bottom half of a toasted bun.
5. Top each patty with a slice of American cheese, crisp bacon, a fried egg, and a hash brown.
6. Serve and enjoy with a dollop of your favorite sauce.

BEEF SHORT RIB, TOMATO, AND POTATO STEW

(TOTAL COOK TIME 8 HOURS 30 MINUTES)

INGREDIENTS FOR 4-8 SERVINGS

THE MEAT

- Beef short ribs (8-lbs, 3.6-kgs)

THE RUB

- Paprika – 1½ cups
- Sugar – ½ cup
- Sea salt – ½ cup
- Freshly ground black pepper – ½ cup
- Chili powder – 4 tablespoons
- Paprika powder – 4 tablespoons
- Garlic powder – 4 tablespoons
- Onion powder – 4 tablespoons
- Olive oil – 4 tablespoons

THE INGREDIENTS

- Olive oil – 1½ tablespoons
- 2 medium-size onion, chopped
- 4 cloves garlic, peeled and minced
- 2 cans of Roma tomatoes (28-ozs, 794-gms) each
- Red wine – 2 cups
- 2 cans of tomato paste (8-ozs, 227-gms) each
- Herbs de Provence – 2 teaspoons
- Worcestershire sauce – 2 tablespoons
- 4 large-sized russet potatoes, peeled and cubed

THE SMOKE

- Preheat your smoker, for indirect smoking to 210°F (99°C)
- Pecan wood chips are recommended for this recipe

METHOD

1. Combine the rub ingredients in a bowl; paprika, sugar, sea salt, freshly ground black pepper, chili powder, paprika powder, garlic powder onion powder, and olive oil.
2. Apply the rub all over the beef short ribs and set aside for 30 minutes.
3. Add the beef short ribs to the smoker and smoke for 4 hours.
4. Meanwhile, prepare the sauce: In a pan, heat the olive oil. Add the onions along with the garlic to the pan and cook until softened.
5. Add the Roma tomatoes to a food blender and process until silky smooth.
6. Transfer the tomato mixture to a pot.
7. Add the softened garlic and onions along with the red wine, tomato paste, Herbs de Provence, and Worcestershire sauce. Bring to boil before reducing the heat and simmering for 30 minutes.
8. Remove the pot from the heat and put to one side.
9. After 4 hours, remove the ribs from the smoker.
10. Add the ribs to a large saucepan.
11. Pour the sauce over the beef short ribs and cover the pan. Add the pan to the smoker and smoke at 250°F (121°C) for 3-4 hours.
12. Add the potatoes to the pan during the final 1½ hours of smoking.
13. Remove from the smoker and serve.

SPAGHETTI BOLOGNESE

(TOTAL COOK TIME 1 HOUR 30 MINUTES)

INGREDIENTS FOR 4 SERVINGS

THE MEAT

- Ground beef (2-lbs, 0.9-kgs)

THE INGREDIENTS

- Extra-virgin olive oil – 1 tablespoon
- 3 garlic cloves, peeled and minced
- 1 yellow onion, peeled and diced
- 3 Roma tomatoes, chopped
- Tomato sauce, store-bought – 2 cups
- Dried oregano – 2 teaspoons
- Dried basil – 1 teaspoon
- Paprika – 2 teaspoons
- Salt and freshly ground black pepper
- Spaghetti (8-ozs, 0.27-kgs)
- Salted butter – 1 tablespoon
- Parmesan cheese, freshly grated, to serve

THE SMOKE

- Preheat the smoker to 225°F (107°C)
- Use apple wood pellets for this recipe

METHOD

1. Heat the olive oil in a deep-sided pan.
2. Add the ground beef along with garlic and onion to the pan. Sauté the meat until no pink remains, it is browned all over and, and the onions soften.
3. Add the chopped tomatoes followed by the tomato sauce, oregano, basil, and paprika. Season with salt and freshly ground black pepper. Stir well to thoroughly combine.
4. Bring to a simmer for 5 minutes while occasionally stirring to avoid the sauce sticking.
5. Remove the pan for the stovetop and transfer it to the preheated smoker. Smoke for 60-90 minutes while stirring occasionally.
6. Meanwhile, cook the spaghetti according to the package instructions and until al dente. Drain well.
7. Once the Bolognese sauce is ready, remove it from the smoker and stir in the butter until melted.
8. Ladle the sauce over the drained pasta.
9. Garnish with freshly grated Parmesan cheese and enjoy.

HONEY-APPLE BBQ RIBS

(TOTAL COOK TIME 2 HOURS 40 MINUTES)

INGREDIENTS FOR 4-6 SERVINGS

THE MEAT

- 4 slabs baby back ribs

THE RUB

- Paprika – ½ cup
- Brown sugar - ⅔ cup
- Onion powder – 2 tablespoons
- Garlic powder - ⅓ cup
- Cayenne pepper – 1 tablespoon
- Chili powder – 2 tablespoons
- White pepper – 1 tablespoon
- Black pepper – 1 tablespoon
- Ground cumin – 1½ teaspoons
- Dried oregano – 1½ teaspoons

THE BASTE

- White grape juice – ½ cup
- Apple juice – ½ cup
- Honey
- BBQ sauce

THE GRILL

- When ready to cook, start your pellet grill on smoke with the lid open to establish the fire
- Preheat to a temperature of 275°F (135°C) with the lid closed

METHOD

1. First, prepare the rub. Combine the paprika, brown sugar, onion powder, garlic powder, cayenne pepper, chili powder, white pepper, black pepper, cumin, and oregano.
2. Sprinkle the rub mixture evenly over the ribs on both sides.
3. Place the ribs on the hot grill, close the lid and cook for 45 minutes.
4. In the meantime, stir together the grape and apple juice and set to one side.
5. Take the ribs off the grill and transfer to a disposable aluminum tray lined with aluminum kitchen foil.
6. Pour the grape-apple juice over the ribs. Drizzle a generous amount of honey over the rubs. Wrap the ribs with the foil, sealing the edges tightly.
7. Return the ribs to the grill and cook for another hour.
8. Take the ribs out of the foil and place directly on the grates. Increase the heat to 350°F (175°C) and cook for another half an hour.
9. Brush the ribs with lashings of BBQ sauce, grill for a final 5 minutes before transferring to a chopping board to rest for 10 minutes.
10. Slice into single servings and enjoy.

CHAPTER 5
CHICKEN

APPLE-WOOD SMOKED CHICKEN BURGERS

(TOTAL COOK TIME 30 MINUTES)

INGREDIENTS FOR 4 SERVINGS

THE POULTRY

- Ground chicken (2-lbs, 0.9-kgs)

THE INGREDIENTS

- 6 green onions, thinly sliced
- Breadcrumbs – 1 cup
- BBQ sauce, store-bought – ½ cup
- Ground oregano – 1 teaspoon
- Garlic powder – 1 teaspoon
- Paprika – 1 teaspoon
- Salt – 1 teaspoon
- Freshly ground black pepper – ½ teaspoon
- Cayenne pepper – ¼ teaspoon
- 4 hamburger buns, split, to serve
- 4 Iceberg lettuce leaves, to serve
- 4 slices of beefsteak tomatoes, to serve
- Red onion slices, to serve

THE SMOKE

- Preheat your smoker to 250°F (121°C)
- Apple wood pellets are recommended for this recipe

METHOD

1. In a mixing bowl, using your hands, combine the chicken along with the green onions, breadcrumbs, BBQ sauce, oregano, garlic powder, paprika, salt, freshly ground black pepper, and cayenne pepper.
2. Shape the mixture into 4 evenly-sized patties and gently flatten.
3. In a single layer, arrange the patties on the smoker racks and smoke until their internal temperature registers 165°F (74°C).
4. Add a lettuce leaf to the bottom half of the bun. Place the chicken burger on top of the lettuce, followed by a slice of tomato and a couple of red onion rings.
5. Cover with the remaining bun halves and enjoy.

APRICOT CHIPOTLE GLAZED CHICKEN

(TOTAL COOK TIME 1 HOUR 5 MINUTES)

INGREDIENTS FOR 2 SERVINGS

THE POULTRY

- 8-12 pieces, skin-on chicken
- Olive oil – ¼ cup
- Granulated garlic – 1 teaspoon
- Salt – ½ teaspoon
- Black pepper – ½ teaspoon

THE GLAZE

- Apricot preserves – ¾ cup
- White wine – ¼ cup
- Chipotle powder – 2 tablespoons

THE SMOKE

- Preheat your wood pellet grill to 365°F (185°C)
- Fruit flavor chips are recommended for this recipe

METHOD

1. Rub the chicken pieces all over with the olive oil, garlic, salt, and black pepper.
2. In a small-size bowl, combine the apricot preserves with the wine, and chipotle powder. Put aside.
3. Cook the chicken on the grill and cook for 25 minutes, or until it registers an internal temperature of 145°F (63 °C).
4. Using a basting brush, liberally brush the glaze from Step 2 all over the chicken.
5. Close the grill and cook the chicken while brushing with more glaze and turning as needed for 10-15 minutes, or internal it registers an internal temperature of 165°F (74°C).
6. Serve and enjoy.

HONEY GINGER HOT CHICKEN WINGS

(TOTAL COOK TIME 55 MINUTES)

INGREDIENTS FOR 4-6 SERVINGS

THE POULTRY

- Chicken wings (3-lbs, 1.36-kgs)
- 2 green onions, thinly sliced diagonally

THE SAUCE

- Soy sauce – ¼ cup
- Honey – ½ cup
- Thumb of ginger, peeled, and finely minced
- 4 garlic cloves, peeled and minced
- Sriracha sauce, to taste
- BBQ sauce, store-bought
- Nonstick cooking spray

THE SMOKE

- Preheat your wood pellet grill to 375°f (190°c)
- Oak or alder wood chips are recommended for this recipe

METHOD

1. First, make the sauce: In a bowl, combine the soy sauce with the honey, ginger, and garlic. Season with Sriracha sauce, to taste, followed by BBQ sauce, again to taste. Mix to combine and toss the chicken wings in half of the sauce.
2. Arrange the wings on a pan lined with aluminum foil. Spray the foil with nonstick spray. The wings must not touch one another.
3. Put the pan on the center of the low rack. Close the lid and bake for 15 minutes.
4. Baste the wings with the remaining sauce and bake for an additional 15 minutes, until they are crisp and register an internal temperature of 165°F (74°C).
5. Remove from the grill and garnish with green onions.

RED CURRY MARINATED CHICKEN

(TOTAL COOK TIME 1 HOUR)

INGREDIENTS FOR 6 SERVINGS

THE POULTRY

- Pieces of chicken (3-lbs, 1.36-kgs)

THE MARINADE

- Red curry paste – 6 teaspoons
- Brown sugar – 1 tablespoon
- Thai fish sauce – 1 tablespoon
- Coconut milk – 3 tablespoons
- Granulated garlic – 1 tablespoon
- Olive oil – 2 tablespoons
- Freshly ground black pepper

THE INGREDIENTS

- Dry white wine – ½ cup
- Fresh cilantro, chopped
- Fresh wedges of lime, to garnish

THE SMOKE

- Set the wood pellet grill to 350°F (177°C)
- Load the smoker with your choice of wood chips

METHOD

1. First, prepare the marinade. In a bowl, combine the red curry paste with the brown sugar, Thai fish sauce, coconut milk, granulated garlic, and olive oil. Season with black pepper.
2. Rub the marinade all over the pieces of chicken, cover, and transfer to the fridge for 60 minutes.
3. Transfer the marinated chicken to an ovenproof pan pour in the white wine.
4. Cover with aluminum foil and grill for 20 minutes.
5. Remove the chicken from the pan. Discard the white wine and over direct heat, grill for an additional 10 minutes. Brush any remaining curry chicken over the chicken.
6. Garnish with cilantro and serve w2ith wedges of lime.

CHAPTER 6
TURKEY

SMOKED WILD TURKEY JERKY

(TOTAL COOK TIME 16 HOURS 10 MINUTES)

INGREDIENTS FOR 8-12 SERVINGS

THE POULTRY

- Turkey breast, thinly sliced (3-lbs, 1.35-kgs)

THE MARINADE

- Soy sauce – 2 cups
- Brown sugar – 1 cup
- 5 cloves of garlic, peeled and chopped
- Fresh ginger, peeled and chopped
- Ground black pepper – 1 tablespoon
- Honey – 3 tablespoons

THE SMOKE

- When you ready to smoke, preheat the smoker with the lid closed for 15 minutes to 180°F (82°C)
- Use cherry wood chips for this recipe

METHOD

1. First, prepare the marinade by combining the soy sauce, brown sugar, garlic, ginger, black pepper, and honey in a ziplock bag.
2. Add the turkey and massage to combine.
3. Transfer the bag to a bowl and place in the fridge for 12-24 hours.
4. When you are ready to cook, remove the turkey from the fridge, shaking over any excess marinade.
5. Arrange the strips of turkey on the grill and allow to smoke for 4 hours, until the jerky is dry.
6. Serve and enjoy.

TURKEY MADRAS

(TOTAL COOK TIME 2 HOURS 20 MINUTES)

INGREDIENTS FOR 6 SERVINGS

THE POULTRY

- 16-18 turkey thighs
- Extra-virgin olive oil
- Basmati rice or Naan bread, to serve
- Coriander, chopped, to serve

THE SAUCE

- Butter, divided (1-lb, 0.45-gms)
- Lemongrass – 2 tablespoons
- Garlic, peeled and minced – ¼ cup
- Fresh ginger, peeled and minced – 2 tablespoons
- Red onion, peeled and thinly sliced
- Madras curry powder – 2 teaspoons
- Garam Masala – 1 teaspoon
- Chicken stock (1-qt, 1-ltr)

THE SMOKE

- Preheat your smoker to 300°F (148°C)

METHOD

1. Grease the turkey thighs all over with olive oil
2. Grill the turkey thighs for approximately 90 minutes. You will need to turn the thighs over every 20-25 minutes. The turkey is good to go when the juices run clear, the outsides are golden brown, and the meat registers an internal temperature of 170°F (77°C).
3. Take the turkey out of the smoker and set aside to rest and cool. Chop into bite-sized pieces.
4. In a saucepan, combine approximately half of the butter together with the lemongrass, minced garlic, minced ginger, and red onions and sauté until golden brown and bite tender.
5. Next, add the Madras curry powder (to taste) along with the garam masala. Turn the heat down and simmer the curry sauce until fragrant and thickened.
6. Pour in the stock and continuing cooking until it reduces by around ¾ of its original volume.
7. Next, stir the turkey meat into the curry sauce.
8. Gradually, add the remaining butter, while stirring, and combing as it cooks.
9. Simmer for 10 minutes before garnishing with chopped coriander.
10. Serve with Basmati rice or Naan bread.

TURKEY MEATLOAF WITH GREEN CHILIES

(TOTAL COOK TIME 2 HOURS 15 MINUTES)

INGREDIENTS FOR 6-8 SERVINGS

THE POULTRY

- Ground turkey (2-lbs, 0.9-kgs)
- Ground turkey chorizo (1-lb, 0.45-kgs)

THE INGREDIENTS

- 1 large size yellow onion, peeled and chopped
- Extra-virgin olive oil – 2 tablespoons
- Sea salt – ½ teaspoon
- Freshly ground black pepper – ½ teaspoon
- Cumin – 1 teaspoon
- Worcestershire sauce – 1 teaspoon
- Chicken stock – ¼ cup
- Tomato paste – 1 tablespoon
- Plain dry breadcrumbs – ¾ cup
- 2 cans diced green chilies, un-drained (4-ozs, 113.4-gms)
- 2 large size eggs, beaten
- Ketchup - ¾ cup

THE SMOKE

- Preheat your smoker for indirect cooking to 325° F (163°C)
- Choose your favorite wood pellets for this recipe

METHOD

1. Over moderate-low heat, in a frying pan, cook the onions along with the olive oil, salt, black pepper, and cumin until the onion is translucent but not browned; this will take approximately 10 minutes.
2. Add the Worcestershire sauce, stock, and tomato paste, mixing until entirely combined. Set aside to cool.
3. In a mixing bowl, combine the ground turkey with the turkey chorizo, breadcrumbs, chilies, eggs, and onion mixture.
4. Mix well to incorporate and shake into an ungreased loaf pan.
5. Evenly spread the ketchup over the top.
6. Cook the meatloaf for 1½ -2 hours or until the internal temperature of the meatloaf registers 160°F (71°C).
7. Allow the meatloaf to rest for several minutes.
8. Slice and serve.

CHAPTER 7
FISH

FENNEL & SWEET PEPPER STUFFED SMOKED TROUT

(TOTAL COOK TIME 45 MINUTES)

INGREDIENTS FOR 4 SERVINGS

THE FISH

- 4 whole trout, deboned, gutted, and prepared for stuffing

THE INGREDIENTS

- Sea salt – 2 teaspoons
- Freshly cracked black pepper – 2 teaspoons
- 8 small sweet red peppers, sliced into strips
- 1 fennel plant, sliced
- Butter, chilled and sliced – ½ cup
- Extra-virgin olive oil – 2 tablespoons
- Lemon wedges, to serve

THE SMOKE

- Preheat your smoker grill to 250°F (121°C)
- Oak or alder wood pellets work well with this recipe

METHOD

1. Season the trout with salt and pepper.
2. Place the trout, side by side, on a baking sheet.
3. Stuff the trout cavities from head to tail with the sweet peppers and sliced fennel.
4. Divide the butter between the cavities
5. Place the trout on the grill and smoke for 30-45 minutes, until the fish flakes easily when using a fork and registers an internal temperature of 145°F (63°C).
6. Drizzle the fish with olive oil, garnish with lemon wedges and enjoy.

LINGCOD WITH CHERRY TOMATOES AND OLIVES

(TOTAL COOK TIME 50 MINUTES)

INGREDIENTS FOR 4-6 SERVINGS

THE FISH

- Fresh lingcod fillets (2-lbs, 0.9-kgs)

THE INGREDIENTS

- Olive oil – ½ cup
- 1 fresh lemon

- 3 garlic cloves, peeled and minced
- Fresh thyme – 1 teaspoon
- Fresh dill – 1 teaspoon
- Sea salt – 1 teaspoon
- 6-8 mini sweet bell peppers, thinly sliced
- 2 small size yellow squash, thinly sliced
- 1½ cups cherry tomatoes, halved
- ⅔ cup Kalamata olives, pitted and halved
- Fresh basil, to serve

THE SMOKE

- Preheat the smoker to 350°F (177°C).
- Mesquite wood chips work well for this recipe

METHOD

1. Slather the cod in olive oil, freshly squeezed juice and zest of ½ lemon, garlic, thyme, dill, and sea salt. Transfer the fish to an oven-safe casserole dish.
2. Slice the remaining ½ lemon into 3 circles and place the rounds evenly on top of the fish.
3. Toss the sweet bell pepper with the squash, tomatoes, and olives and scatter them over the fish.
4. Smoke the fish for 35 minutes, or until it flakes easily when using a fork.
5. Scatter with fresh basil and serve.

MAPLE SMOKED RED SNAPPER STEAKS

(TOTAL COOK TIME 2 HOURS 40 MINUTES)

INGREDIENTS FOR 4 SERVINGS

THE FISH

- Snapper steaks (2-lbs, 0.9-kgs)

THE INGREDIENTS

- Extra-virgin olive oil – 4 tablespoons
- 1 clove of garlic, peeled and minced
- Sea salt – ½ teaspoon

- Black pepper – ⅛ teaspoon
- Freshly squeezed lemon juice – 2 tablespoons
- Dry white wine – ½ cup
- Dried tarragon – ½ teaspoon
- Fresh chives, finely chopped – 1 tablespoon
- 2 fresh lemons, cut into wedges
- Fresh parsley, chopped

THE SMOKE

- Preheat your smoker to 220-250°F (100-120°C)
- Choose maple pellets for this recipe

METHOD

1. For the marinade: In a mixing bowl, combine the olive oil with the minced garlic, sea salt, black pepper, freshly squeezed lemon juice, dry white wine, dried tarragon, and chopped chives.
2. Place the snapper steaks in a shallow glass bowl.
3. Pour the marinade evenly over the top, cover, and place in the refrigerator for 1 hour.
4. Remove from the refrigerator and put aside to rest for 20-25 minutes.
5. Remove the snapper steaks from the marinade, shaking off any excess marinade and cook in the smoker for 60 minutes. The fish is cooked through when it flakes easily when using a fork. It is important to take care not to overcook.
6. Serve with a squeeze of fresh lemon juice and garnish with parsley.

CHAPTER 8
SEAFOOD

BARBECUE SHRIMP

(TOTAL COOK TIME 25 MINUTES)

INGREDIENTS FOR 2-3 SERVINGS

THE SEAFOOD

- 12 jumbo shrimp, rinsed and patted dry

THE SAUCE

- Olive oil, divided – 1½ tablespoons
- Sea salt and coarsely ground black pepper
- ½ small-size onion, peeled and thinly sliced
- 1 clove of garlic, peeled and minced
- ½ jalapeno pepper, seeded and finely minced
- Barbecue sauce, store-bought – ½ cup
- Fresh cilantro leaves, finely chopped

THE SMOKE

- When you are ready to start cooking, and with the lid open, on smoke, establish the fire for 5 minutes
- Close the smoker's lid and preheat to 450°F (220°C) for 12-15 minutes
- Hickory wood chips are recommended for this recipe

METHOD

1. Add the shrimp to a large mixing bowl and add 1 tablespoon of the olive oil. Generously season with sea salt and freshly ground black pepper, and set to one side while you prepare the sauce.
2. Over moderate-low heat, in a saucepan, warm the remaining oil.
3. Add the onion to the pan, followed by the garlic and jalapeno pepper. Sauté until softened.
4. Add the barbecue sauce, stirring to combine, and keep the sauce warm.
5. Arrange the shrimp on the grill grate in the smoker and cook on each side for 2-3 minutes, until the shrimp and firm and opaque.
6. Fold the cooked shrimp into the barbecue sauce.
7. Stir in the chopped cilantro and enjoy.

CRAB AND SHRIMP DIP

(TOTAL COOK TIME 30 MINUTES)

INGREDIENTS FOR 4-6 SERVINGS

THE SEAFOOD

- Lump crab meat, shredded (4-ozs, 113-gms)
- Fresh raw shrimp, peeled, deveined, and chopped (8-ozs, 0.22-kgs)

THE INGREDIENTS

- 3 cloves of garlic, peeled and minced
- Sea salt – ¼ teaspoon
- Butter – 1-2 tablespoons
- 1 onion, peeled and thinly sliced
- Green bell pepper, finely sliced – ½ cup
- Celery, trimmed and finely diced – ¼ cup
- Jalapeno, minced – 1 tablespoon
- Spinach, chopped – ½ cup
- Old Bay seasoning – 1 teaspoon
- Cream cheese, softened – ½ cup
- Gouda cheese, unsmoked and freshly grated – 3 cups
- Gruyere cheese – ½ cup
- Paprika, to season
- French baguette, sliced, to serve

THE SMOKE

- Preheat your smoker to 250°F (121°C)

METHOD

1. In a small bowl, mash the minced garlic with the sea salt.
2. Melt the butter in a skillet. Add the onion along with the green bell pepper, celery, and jalapeno and sauté until fork tender.
3. Add the spinach followed by the smashed seasoned garlic and Old Bay seasoning. Stir well to entirely combine and until the spinach has wilted.
4. Next, add crab and shrimp and cook for 60 seconds, until the shrimp becomes opaque.
5. Remove the skillet from the heat and stir in the cream cheese followed by the Gouda, Gruyere cheeses. Add a sprinkling of paprika to season.
6. Transfer the pan to the smoker and cook for approximately 15 minutes, or until the dip is bubbling and golden.
7. Remove the skillet from the smoker and serve with slices of French baguette.

SCALLOP PASTA

(TOTAL COOK TIME 1 HOUR)

INGREDIENTS FOR 4 SERVINGS

THE SEAFOOD

- 16 scallops, rinsed and prepared

THE INGREDIENTS

- Dry linguine pasta (8-ozs, 227-gms)
- Vegetable oil, divided – 4 tablespoons
- 2 shallots, finely diced
- 4 garlic cloves peeled and minced
- ½ medium-size onion, peeled and sliced
- Dry white wine – 6 tablespoons
- Butter – 4 tablespoons
- Salt and freshly ground black pepper, to season
- 16 cherry tomatoes, halved
- Parmesan cheese, freshly shredded – ½ cup
- Fresh parsley, chopped – 4 tablespoons
- Lemon wedges, to serve

THE SMOKE

- Preheat, the smoker to 150°F (65°C)
- Alder wood chips are recommended for this recipe

METHOD

1. Add the prepared scallops to a disposable aluminum tray, place in the smoker, and smoke for 30-45 minutes.
2. Meanwhile, bring a saucepan of salted water to boil and cook the linguine until al dente. Drain and rinse the pasta under running water. Put to one side.
3. Toss the drained linguine in 1 tablespoon olive oil.
4. Heat the remaining olive oil in a pan on medium heat.
5. Add the shallots followed by the garlic and onions. Cook for 3-5 minutes, or until the onions are translucent.
6. Deglaze the pan with the dry white wine.
7. Add the pasta and the smoked scallops to the pan and entirely combine.
8. Stir in the butter and season with salt and black pepper.
9. Scatter the cherry tomatoes over the pasta, scatter with cheese and garnish with fresh parsley and lemon wedges.

CHAPTER 9
VEGETABLES

GERMAN-STYLE SAUERKRAUT WITH APPLES

(TOTAL COOK TIME 45 MINUTES)

INGREDIENTS FOR 4 SERVINGS

THE VEGETABLES

- Sauerkraut, rinsed and drained (2-lbs, 0.9-kgs)
- Chicken broth – 1½ cups
- White wine – ½ cup
- Caraway seeds – 1 teaspoon
- 1 large size red apple, cored and thinly sliced

THE GRILL

- With the lid closed, preheat The grill to 375°F (135°C)
- Add apple flavor wood chips

METHOD

1. Add the sauerkraut to an ovenproof, oval-shaped casserole dish.
2. Stir in the remaining ingredients (chicken broth, white wine, caraway, and apple) to combine.
3. When the grill is heated, cook for 40-50 minutes until the edges of the sauerkraut are browned, and the slices of apple are bite-tender.

GRILLED BROCCOLI WITH LIME BUTTER

(TOTAL COOK TIME 20 MINUTES)

INGREDIENTS FOR 4 SERVINGS

THE VEGETABLES

- 2 large size broccoli heads, trimmed, cut into florets
- Olive oil – 2 tablespoons
- Salt – ½ teaspoon
- Queso fresco, crumbled, to serve

THE LIME BUTTER

- Butter, softened – 3 tablespoons
- Freshly squeezed juice and zest of ½ large size lime
- Red pepper sauce – 1 teaspoon
- Runny honey – 2 teaspoons

THE GRILL

- Preheat the grill to 575°F (301°C) with the lid closed
- Oak wood pellets are a good choice for this recipe

METHOD

1. For the lime butter: In a small size bowl, stir the butter with the lime zest, red pepper sauce, and honey until silky smooth. Put to one side.
2. In a second, large size bowl, stir the florets with the oil and salt.
3. Place the florets directly onto the grill grate, while occasionally turning until slightly charred and crisp-tender, for approximately 8 minutes.
4. Transfer the broccoli to a serving plate and toss evenly with the lime butter.
5. Garnish with queso fresco and enjoy.

GRILLED VEGETABLE SALAD

(TOTAL COOK TIME 25 MINUTES)

INGREDIENTS FOR 2-4 SERVINGS

THE VEGETABLES

- Asparagus, trimmed (8-ozs, 227-gms)
- 2 small zucchinis
- 1 red onion, peeled and sliced thick
- 1 red bell pepper, seeded and quartered
- 1 orange red bell pepper, seeded and quartered
- 2 ears of corn, shucked
- 2 romaine lettuce hearts, halved lengthwise and shredded

THE DRESSING

- Balsamic vinegar – ¼ cup
- Dijon mustard – 1 tablespoon
- 2 garlic cloves, peeled and minced
- Salt and freshly ground black pepper, to taste

THE GRILL

- Preheat your grill to 600°F (315° C)
- Once heated, set to cook on open flame mode
- Use the direct flame insert

METHOD

1. Arrange all the vegetables (asparagus, zucchini, onion, red pepper, orange peppers, and corn) on the lower rack of the hot grill.
2. Cook until the veggies are slightly charred and bite-tender. You will need to turn the vegetables occasionally while they are grilling for 10-15 minutes. Each type of vegetable will have a different grill time, so remove them from the grill as they cook.
3. Cut the grilled large-size vegetable into bite-size pieces.
4. Add the lettuce to a serving plate.
5. Place the chunks of grilled vegetables over the lettuce.
6. Slice the corn off the cob and scatter it over the top.
7. To prepare the dressing: In a bowl, whisk the vinegar with the mustard and garlic—season with salt and black pepper to taste and whisk to combine.
8. Serve the salad while it is warm and with the dressing on the side.

CHAPTER 10
GAME

FROG LEGS WITH CREOLE DIPPING SAUCE

(TOTAL COOK TIME 12 HOURS 45 MINUTES)

INGREDIENTS FOR 4 SERVINGS

THE GAME

- Frog legs (2-lbs, 0.9-kgs)

THE MARINADE

- Louisiana hot sauce, store-bought (12-ozs, 340-gms)
- Black pepper – 2 tablespoons
- Salt – 1 tablespoon
- Onion powder – 1 tablespoon
- Garlic powder – 1 tablespoon
- Cayenne pepper – 1 tablespoon
- Cornstarch – 1 cup

THE DIPPING SAUCE

- Olive oil – 2 tablespoons
- Butter, unsalted – 2 tablespoons
- Yellow onion, peeled and diced – ½ cup
- Garlic, peeled and minced – 2 tablespoons
- Freshly squeezed lemon juice – 2 tablespoons
- Flat-leaf parsley, chopped – 2 tablespoons
- Heavy whipping cream – 1 cup
- Creole mustard, store-bought – ½ cup

THE SMOKE

- When you are ready to begin cooking, with the lid open, set your grill to smoke and establish the fire, for 4-5 minutes
- Set the temperature of your smoker to 450°F (232°C) and with the lid closed preheat for 10-15 minutes
- Hickory wood pellets are recommended for this recipe

METHOD

1. In a bowl, whisk the marinade ingredients (hot sauce, pepper, salt, onion powder, garlic powder, cayenne pepper, and cornstarch) until combined.
2. Add the frog legs to a large size ziplock bag.
3. Pour the marinade into the bag, and transfer to the fridge for 12-24 hours, to marinate.
4. For the dipping sauce: In a pan, over moderate-high heat, beat the oil with the butter. Add the onion followed by the garlic, fresh lemon juice, and parsley.
5. Sauté until the onions are translucent; this will take approximately 5 minutes.
6. Stir in the cream until it reduces for around 10 minutes.
7. Stir in the mustard until entirely combined. Remove the pan from the heat and keep warm until you are ready to serve.
8. Remove the frog legs from the marinade and arrange them on the grill. Grill for 4 minutes before gently flipping them over and continuing to cook until they register an internal temperature of 160°F (71°C).
9. Remove the frog legs from the grill and serve with a side dish of dipping sauce.

GRILLED DUCK BREAST

(TOTAL COOK TIME 30 MINUTES)

INGREDIENTS FOR 4 SERVINGS

THE GAME

- 4 boneless duck breasts (6-ozs, 170-gms each)
- Big game rub of choice, store-bought – ¼ cup

THE GRILL

- When you are ready to cook, and with the lid closed, preheat the temperature to high for 15 minutes
- Cherry wood pellets are recommended for this recipe

METHOD

1. Score the duck skin with a ¼-ins (0.64-cms) diamond pattern.
2. Season the duck on both sides with your chosen rub.
3. Place the breasts, skin side facing downwards on the grill grate. Close the lid and cook for 15-20 minutes until medium-rare. Using an internal thermometer, the meat should register 130-135°F (54-57°C)
4. Remove the duck from the grill and set aside for 4-5 minutes before slicing against the grain into thick slices.
5. Serve.

ROASTED ELK PEPPER POPPERS

(TOTAL COOK TIME 8 HOURS 50 MINUTES)

INGREDIENTS FOR 10-12 SERVINGS

THE GAME

- 2-4 elk steaks

THE INGREDIENTS

- 20 fresh jalapeno peppers
- Garlic and herb flavor cream cheese (12-ozs, 340-gms)
- 20 slices of bacon, halved

THE MARINADE

- Worcestershire sauce – 1 cup
- Freshly squeezed lime juice –1 cup
- 1 cup soy sauce

THE GRILL

- Preheat with the lid closed to 350°F (177°C) for 15 minutes
- Game specific wood pellets are recommended for this recipe

METHOD

1. First, thinly slice the elk steaks into bite-size pieces roughly the same length and width as the whole peppers.
2. Make a marinade: In a bowl, mix the Worcestershire sauce and lime juice with the soy sauce.
3. Add the slices of elk steak to the bowl and allow to marinate in the fridge overnight.
4. Slice the jalapeno peppers lengthwise in half. Remove their seeds and membrane and arrange on a serving platter, cut side facing upwards.
5. Spoon the cream cheese evenly into the pepper halves.
6. Remove the steak strips for the marinade and gently shake off any excess.
7. Arrange one slice of marinated meat on top of each cheese-filled jalapeño.
8. Wrap each pepper popper in one slice of bacon and secure with a cocktail stick.
9. Place the poppers on the grill, cut side facing upwards, and cook for 10-15 minutes, or until the meat is cooked through and the peppers are lightly charred and bite tender.
10. Remove the cocktail sticks and serve.

CHAPTER 11
SMOKING MEAT

WOOD PELLET USING TIPS

Before starting to use your Wood Pellet for the first time, and before getting started with some of the most sumptuous recipes you can ever stumble into, here are some of the most important things you need to know about Wood Pellets at first. Indeed, Wood pellets are basically a form of compressed wood and of sawdust that is basically created through the process of exposing certain agents to a certain degree of heat. And one of the most well-known uses of wood pellets is to use it in order to fuel certain cooking smokers and grills. Wood Pellet Smokers and Grills are indeed, known for bringing a very special smoked flavour of wood to the food ingredients you are smoking or to any type of meat. And the smoking taste that you can get from wood pellet smokers is very special and unique that you can never forget the taste of food once you try smoke cooking it with the Wood Pellet Smoker or Grill. And before starting your wood pellet journey, here are some tips of using Wood Pellet Smoker or Grills, in addition to some benefits of Wood Pellet cooking:

1. Wood pellets are mainly characterized by being eco-friendly; basically because most of the Wood Pellets are made of renewable elements and materials. The production of Wood Pellets encourages on the process of repurposing the materials that can be thrown away by people.
2. Wood pellets are usually available in various forms and types; each of which can offer a different flavour. And this includes cherry, alder, apple, maple, oak, mesquite and hickory wood pellets

3. Wood pellets are known for being a lot more efficient in comparison to other types of gas and fossil because wood pellets are mainly able to use about 90% of the contained energy. And then the wood pellets can turn the energy into heat.
4. Wood pellets can help you cook some very delicious dishes with the smoky flavour it can offer you. Thanks to Wood Pellet Smoking method, you will be able to enjoy tastes that are similar to that obtained when using charcoal.
5. Wood pellets can help you produce a very nice flavour and you will be able to easily clean you Wood Pellet Smoker or Grill because there won't be so much ash.
6. Whenever you want to use your wood pellet smoker grill, switch on the charcoal grill by firing up a quantity of charcoal. Then wait for the charcoal to heat up before sprinkling an amount of wood pellets under the rock grate.
7. Within a short period of time, your wood pellets will start igniting. And once you see the pellets sparkle it is a signal that you should start cooking and you will see the nice wood smoke. Close the lid of your wood pellet smoker in order to keep the smoke in.
8. While it's okay to use wood pellets on their own, you'll notice that they burn too quickly without the charcoal. And some people choose to use a smoker box or add foil in order to slow down the process of burning. Usually 2/3 cup of wood pellets can give you about ½ hour of smoke.
9. You can use a pellet tube smoker in order to keep wood pellets in as you combine it with the charcoal. And this can help increase the smokiness of the flavour. Pellet tube smokers are usually affordable and are worth to check it out.

Selecting a Smoker

You need to invest in a good smoker if you are going to smoke meat on a regular basis. Consider these options when buying a smoker. Here are two natural fire option for you:

- Charcoal smokers are fueled by a combination of charcoal and wood. Charcoal burns easily and the temperature remains steady, so you won't have any problem with a charcoal smoker. The wood gives a great flavor to the meat and you will enjoy smoking meats.

- Wood smoker: The wood smoker will give your brisket and ribs the best smoky flavor and taste, but it is a bit harder to cook with wood. Both hardwood blocks and chips are used as fuel.

Choose your wood

You need to choose your wood carefully because the type of wood you will use affect greatly to the flavor and taste of the meat. Here are a few options for you:

- Maple: Maple has a smoky and sweet taste and goes well with pork or poultry

- Alder: Alder is sweet and light. Perfect for poultry and fish.

- Apple: Apple has a mild and sweet flavor. Goes well with pork, fish, and poultry.

- Oak: Oak is great for slow cooking. Ideal for game, pork, beef, and lamb.

- Mesquite: Mesquite has a smoky flavor and extremely strong. Goes well with pork or beef.

- Hickory: Has a smoky and strong flavor. Goes well with beef and lamb.

- Cherry Has a mild and sweet flavor. Great for pork, beef, and turkey

Wood Type	Fish	Chicken	Beef	Pork
Apple	Yes	Yes	No	No
Alder	Yes	Yes	No	Yes
Cherry	Yes	Yes	Yes	Yes
Hickory	No	No	Yes	Yes
Maple	No	Yes	No	No
Mulberry	Yes	Yes	No	Yes
Mesquite	No	No	Yes	Yes
Oak	Yes	Yes	Yes	Yes
Pecan	No	Yes	Yes	Yes
Pear	No	Yes	No	Yes
Peach	No	Yes	No	Yes
Walnut	No	No	Yes	Yes

Remember, black smoke is bad and white smoke is good. Ensure proper ventilation for great tasting smoked meat.

Select the right meat

Some meats are just ideal for the smoking process, including:

- Chicken
- Turkey
- Pork roast
- Ham
- Brisket
- Pork and beef ribs
- Corned beef

Find the right temperature

- Start at 250F (120C): Start your smoker a bit hot. This extra heat gets the smoking process going.
- Temperature drop: Once you add the meat to the smoker, the temperature will drop, which is fine.
- Maintain the temperature. Monitor and maintain the temperature. Keep the temperature steady during the smoking process.

Avoid peeking every now and then. Smoke and heat two most important element make your meat taste great. If you open the cover every now and then you lose both of them and your meat loses flavor. Only the lid only when you truly need it.

THE CORE DIFFERENCE BETWEEN COLD AND HOT SMOKING

Depending on the type of grill that you are using, you might be able to get the option to go for a Hot Smoking Method or a Cold Smoking One. The primary fact about these three different cooking techniques which you should keep in mind are as follows:

- **Hot Smoking**: In this technique, the food will use both the heat on your grill and the smoke to prepare your food. This method is most suitable for items such as chicken, lamb, brisket etc.
- **Cold Smoking**: In this method, you are going to smoke your meat at a very low temperature such as 30 degree Celsius, making sure that it doesn't come into the direct contact with the heat. This is mostly used as a means to preserve meat and extend their life on the shelf.
- **Roasting Smoke**: This is also known as Smoke Baking. This process is essentially a combined form of both roasting and baking and can be performed in any type of smoker with a capacity of reaching temperatures above 82 degree Celsius.

THE BASIC PREPARATIONS

- Always be prepared to spend the whole day and take as much time as possible to smoke your meat for maximum effect.
- Make sure to obtain the perfect Ribs/Meat for the meal which you are trying to smoke. Do a little bit of research if you need.
- I have already added a list of woods in this book, consult to that list and choose the perfect wood for your meal.
- Make sure to prepare the marinade for each of the meals properly. A great deal of the flavor comes from the rubbing.
- Keep a meat thermometer handy to get the internal temperature when needed.
- Use mittens or tongs to keep yourself safe
- Refrain yourself from using charcoal infused alongside starter fluid as it might bring a very unpleasant odor to your food
- Always make sure to start off with a small amount of wood and keep adding them as you cook.
- Don't be afraid to experiment with different types of wood for newer flavor and experiences.
- Always keep a notebook near you and note jot down whatever you are doing or learning and use them during the future session. This will help you to evolve and move forward.

THE CORE ELEMENTS OF SMOKING!

Smoking is a very indirect method of cooking that relies on a number of different factors to give you the most perfectly cooked meal that you are looking for. Each of these components is very important to the whole process as they all work together to create the meal of your dreams.

- **Time**: Unlike grilling or even Barbequing, smoking takes a really long time and requires a whole lot of patience. It takes time for the smoky flavor to slowly get infused into the meats. Jus to bring things into comparison, it takes an about 8 minutes to fully cook a steak through direct heating, while smoking (indirect heating) will take around 35-40 minutes.
- **Temperature:** When it comes to smoking, the temperature is affected by a lot of different factors that are not only limited to the wind, cold air temperatures but also the cooking wood's dryness. Some smokers work best with large fires that are controlled by the draw of a chimney and restricted airflow through the various vents of the cooking chamber and firebox. While other smokers tend to require smaller fire with fewer coals as well as a completely different combination of the vent and draw controls. However, most smokers are designed to work at temperatures as low as 180 degrees Fahrenheit to as high as 300 degrees Fahrenheit. But the recommend temperature usually falls between 250 degrees Fahrenheit and 275 degrees Fahrenheit.
- **Airflow:** The level of air to which the fire is exposed to greatly determines how your fire will burn and how quickly it will burn the fuel. For instance, if you restrict air flow into the firebox by closing up the available vents, then the fire will burn at a low temperature and vice versa. Typically in smokers, after lighting up the fire, the vents are opened to allow for maximum airflow and is then adjusted throughout the cooking process to make sure that optimum flame is achieved.
- **Insulation:** Insulation is also very important when it comes to smokers as it helps to easily manage the cooking process throughout the whole cooking session. A good insulation allows smokers to efficiently reach the desired temperature instead of waiting for hours upon hours!

CONCLUSION

The book includes smoked meat recipes comprising beef, fish, seafood, pork, ham, lamb, poultry, vegetables, and game. If you want to just treat yourself to mouthwatering, perfectly cooked smoked meat or entertain family or friends, this book will provide everything you need.

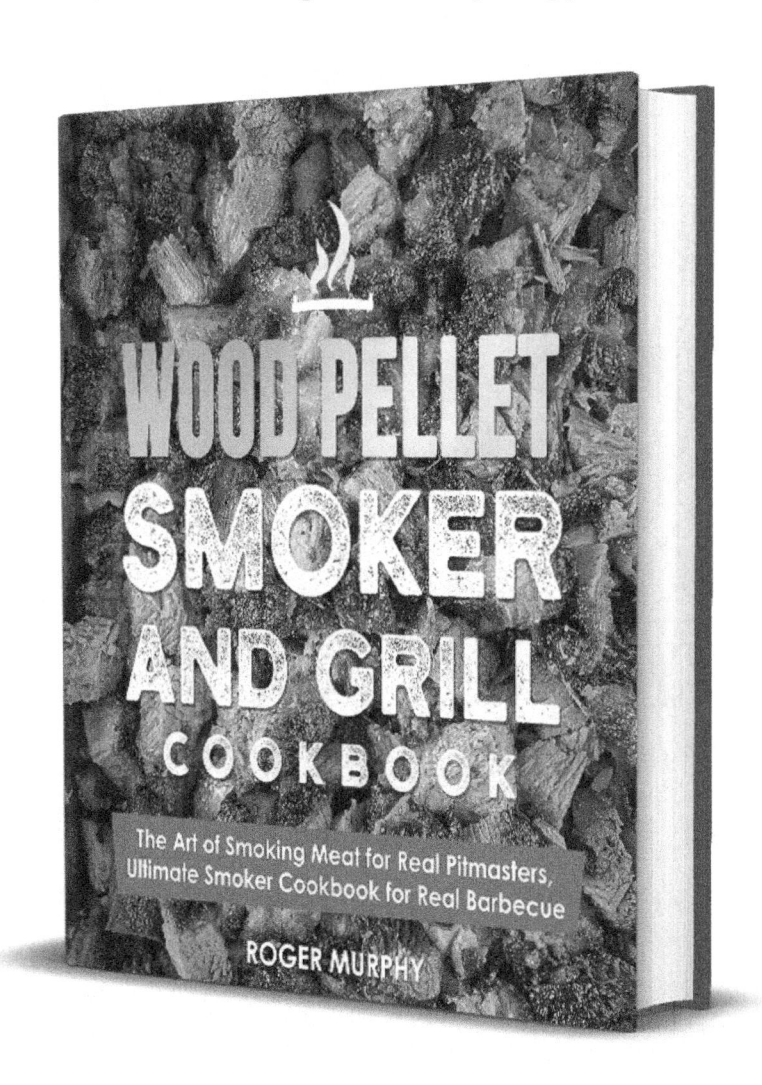

MY BOOKS

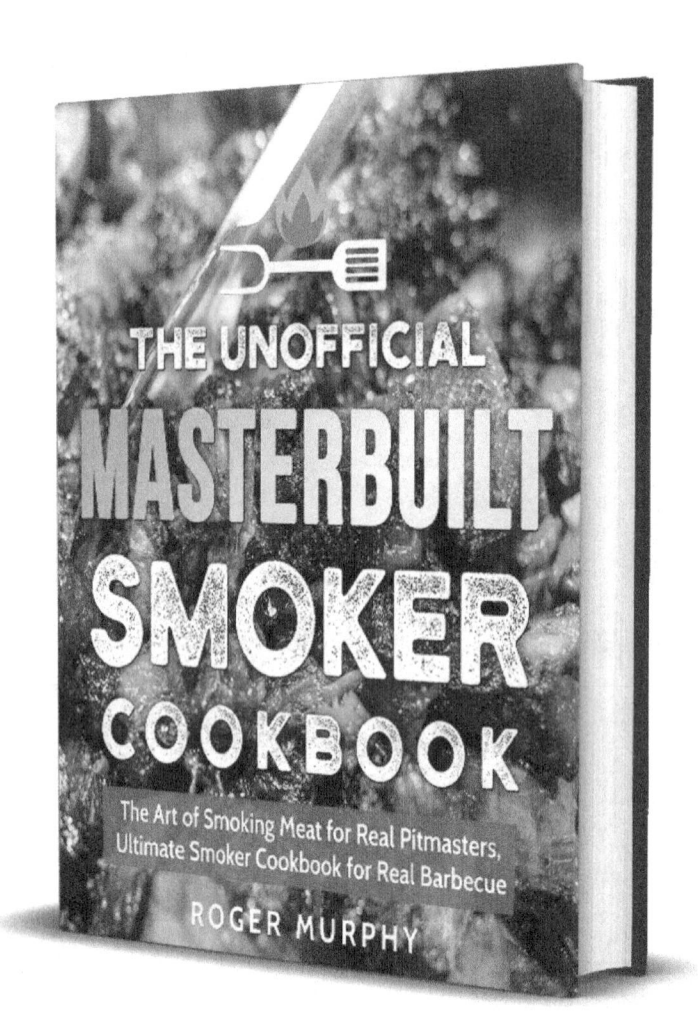

https://www.amazon.com/dp/1797805525

https://www.amazon.com/dp/1708846697

https://www.amazon.com/dp/1703308271

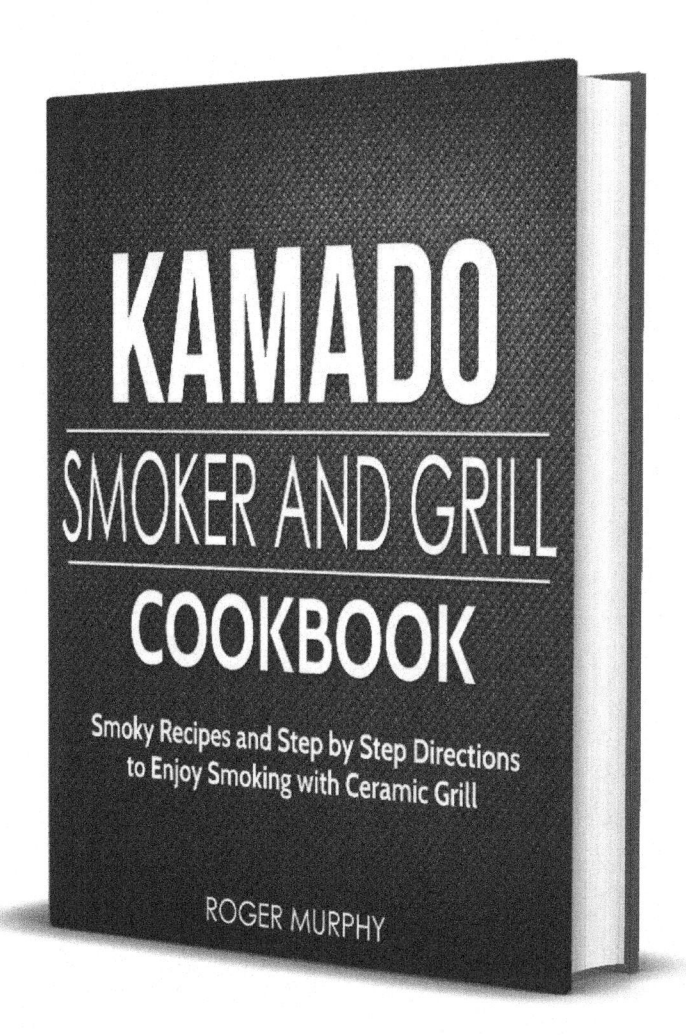

https://www.amazon.com/dp/1070935603

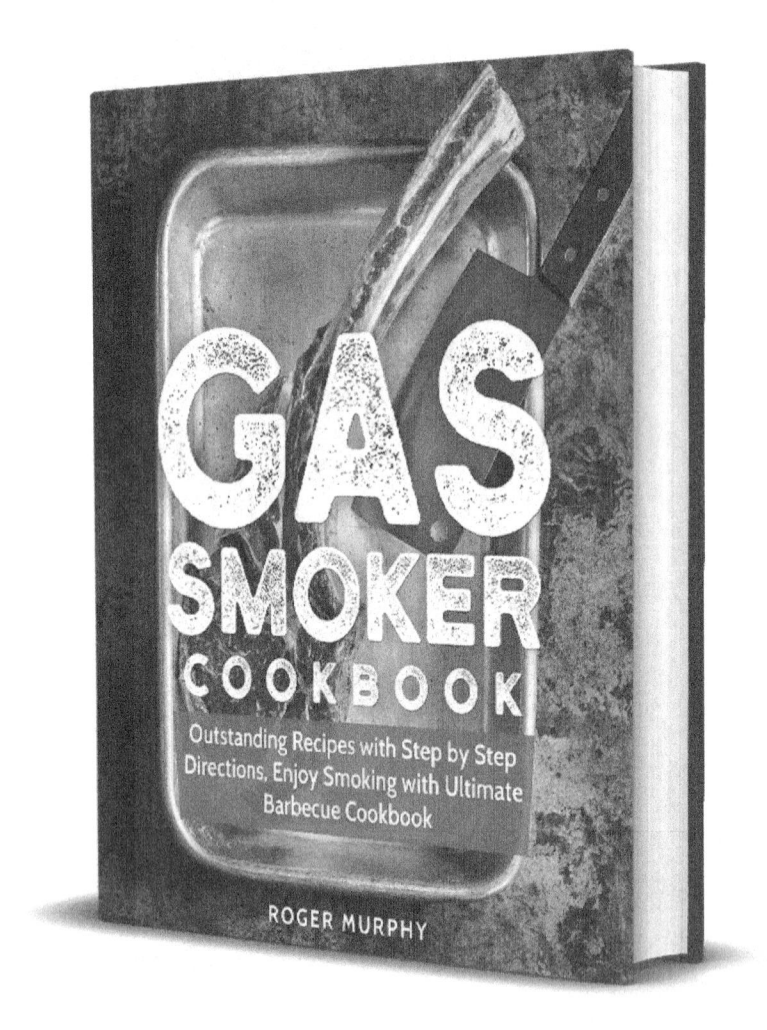

https://www.amazon.com/dp/1088813011

https://www.amazon.com/dp/1096508257

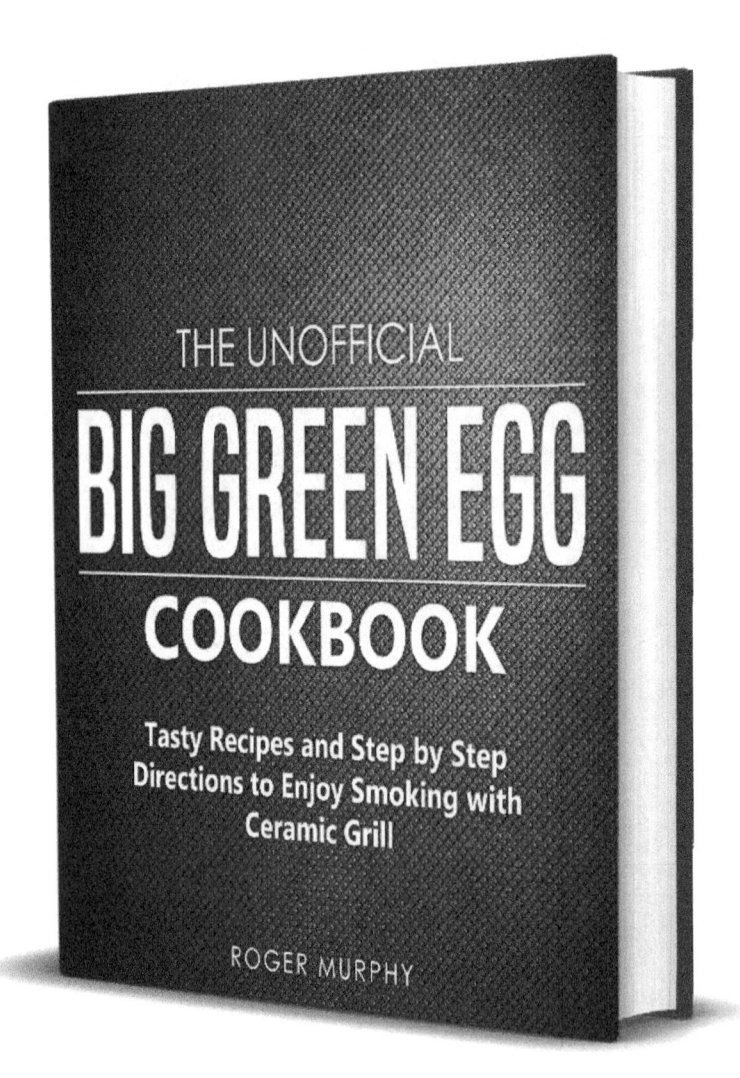

The Unofficial

BIG GREEN EGG
COOKBOOK

Tasty Recipes and Step by Step Directions to Enjoy Smoking with Ceramic Grill

ROGER MURPHY

https://www.amazon.com/dp/1091181322

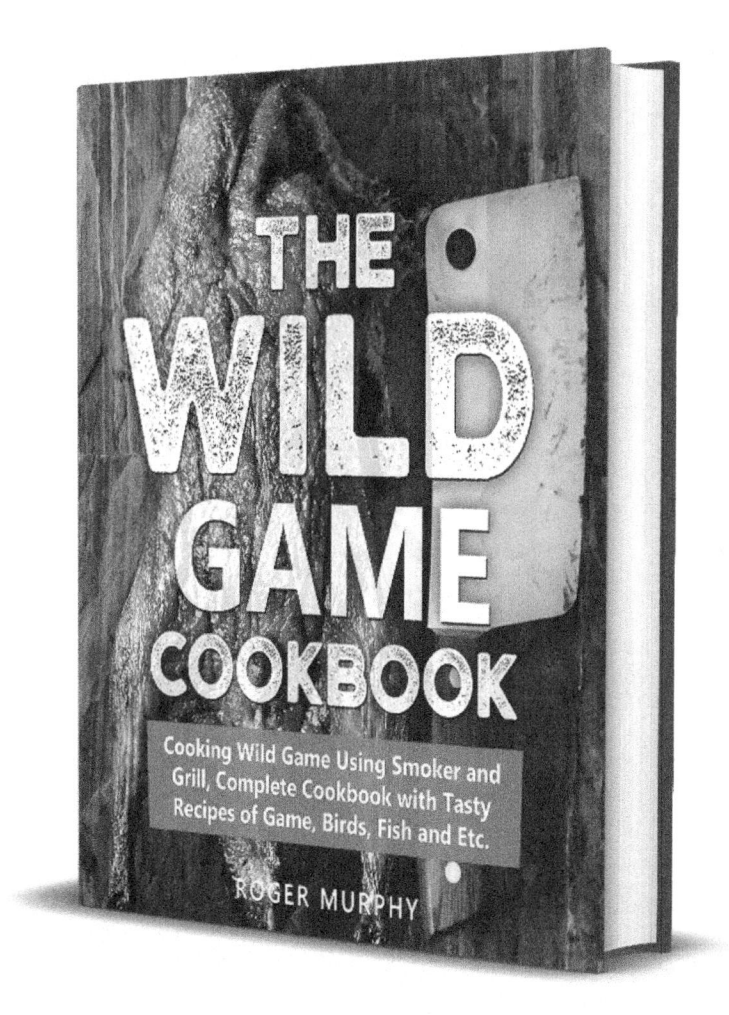

https://www.amazon.com/dp/1696290074

https://www.amazon.com/dp/B07KYWLF13

https://www.amazon.com/dp/1731126360

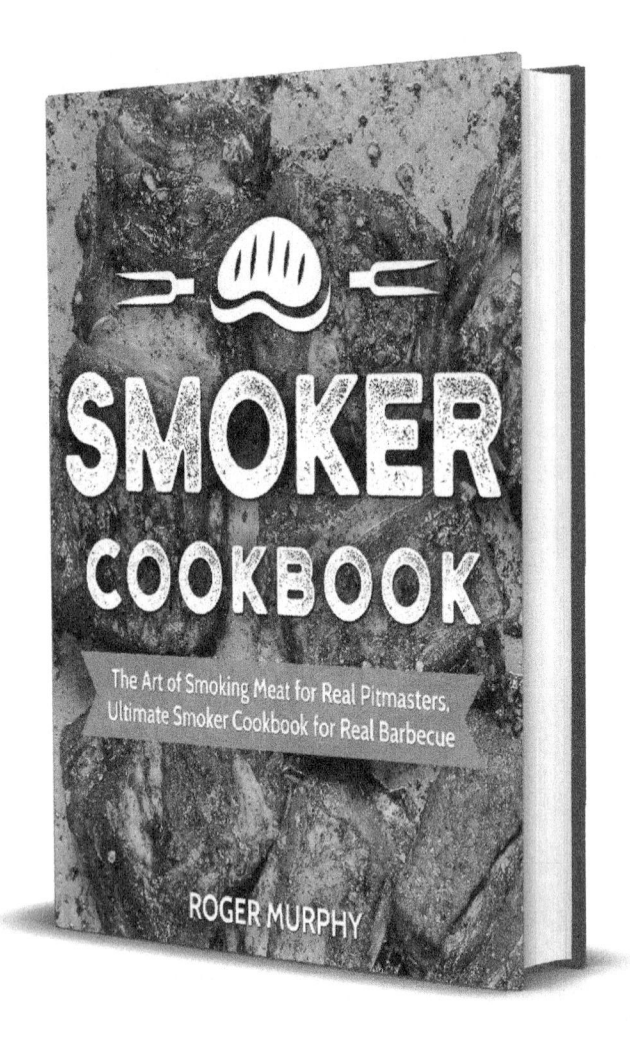

https://www.amazon.com/dp/1731563310

P.S. Thank you for reading this book. If you've enjoyed this book, please don't shy, drop me a line, leave a feedback or both on Amazon. I love reading feedbacks and your opinion is extremely important for me.

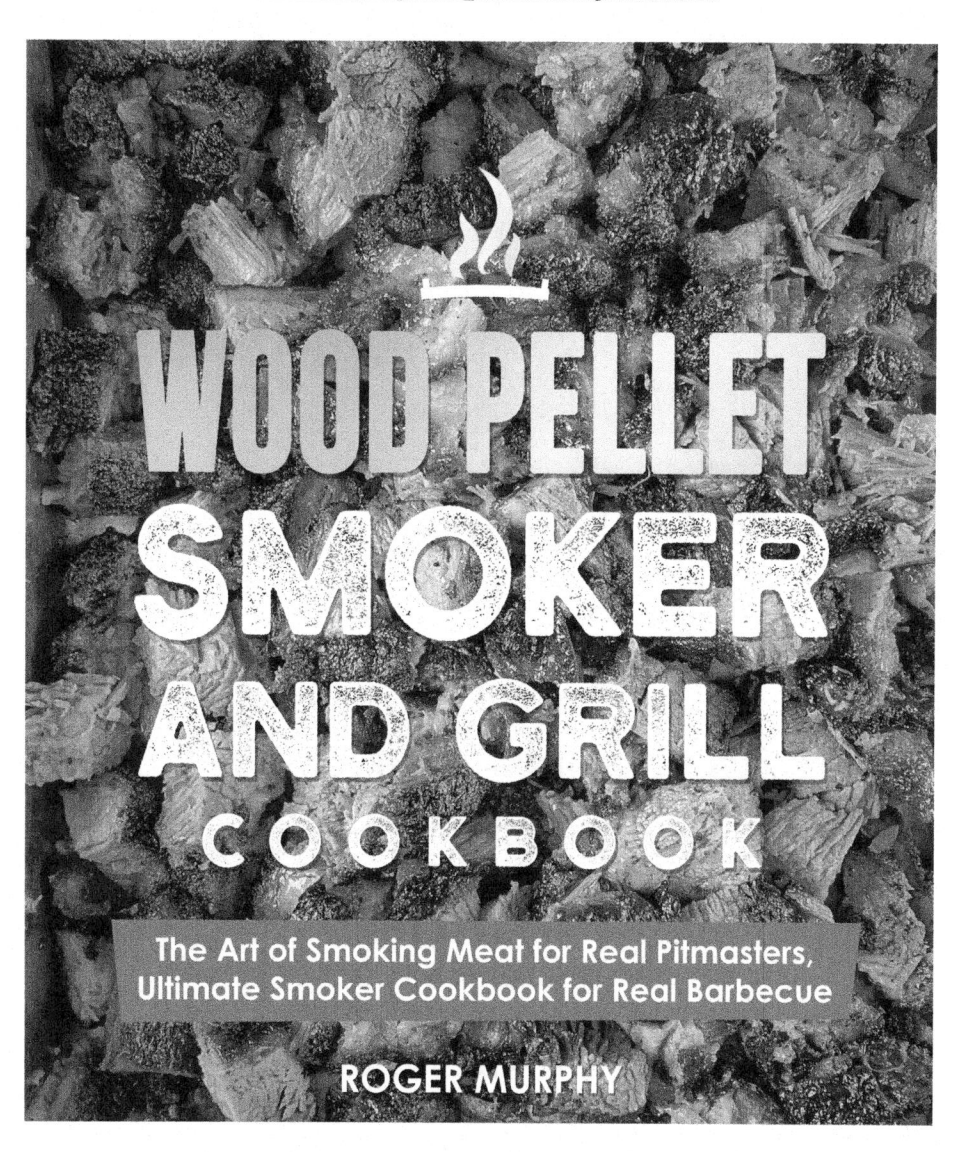

WOOD PELLET SMOKER AND GRILL COOKBOOK

The Art of Smoking Meat for Real Pitmasters, Ultimate Smoker Cookbook for Real Barbecue

ROGER MURPHY

GET YOUR FREE GIFT

Subscribe to our Mail List and get your FREE copy of the book

'Smoking Meat: The Best 20 Recipes of Smoked Meat, Unique Recipes for Unique BBQ'

https://tiny.cc/smoke20

Copyright 2020© Roger Murphy

All rights reserved. No part of this guide may be reproduced in any form without permission in writing from the publisher except in the case of brief quotations embodied in critical articles or reviews.

Legal & Disclaimer: *The information contained in this book and its contents is not designed to replace or take the place of any form of medical or professional advice; and is not meant to replace the need for independent medical, financial, legal or other professional advice or services, as may be required. The content and information in this book have been provided for educational and entertainment purposes only.*

The content and information contained in this book have been compiled from sources deemed reliable, and it is accurate to the best of the Author's knowledge, information, and belief. However, the Author cannot guarantee its accuracy and validity and cannot be held liable for any errors and/or omissions. Further, changes are periodically made to this book as and when needed. Where appropriate and/or necessary, you must consult a professional (including but not limited to your doctor, attorney, financial advisor or such other professional advisor) before using any of the suggested remedies, techniques, or information in this book.

Upon using the contents and information contained in this book, you agree to hold harmless the Author from and against any damages, costs, and expenses, including any legal fees potentially resulting from the application of any of the information provided by this book.

This disclaimer applies to any loss, damages or injury caused by the use and application, whether directly or indirectly, of any advice or information presented, whether for breach of contract, tort, negligence, personal injury, criminal intent, or under any other cause of action.

You agree to accept all risks of using the information presented in this book.

You agree that by continuing to read this book, where appropriate and/or necessary, you shall consult a professional (including but not limited to your doctor, attorney, or financial advisor or such other advisor as needed) before using any of the suggested remedies, techniques, or information in this book.

Made in the USA
Coppell, TX
12 December 2020